You Are Forgiven

David Guy

TEACH Services, Inc.
PUBLISHING
www.TEACHServices.com • (800) 367-1844

World rights reserved. This book or any portion thereof may not be copied or reproduced in any form or manner whatever, except as provided by law, without the written permission of the publisher, except by a reviewer who may quote brief passages in a review.

The author assumes full responsibility for the accuracy of all facts and quotations as cited in this book. The opinions expressed in this book are the author's personal views and interpretations, and do not necessarily reflect those of the publisher.

This book is provided with the understanding that the publisher is not engaged in giving spiritual, legal, medical, or other professional advice. If authoritative advice is needed, the reader should seek the counsel of a competent professional.

Copyright © 2021 TEACH Services, Inc.
Copyright © 2021 David Guy
ISBN-13: 978-1-4796-1311-3 (Paperback)
ISBN-13: 978-1-4796-1312-0 (ePub)
Library of Congress Control Number: 2021914844

Scripture quotations marked (KJV) are taken from the King James Version of the Bible. Public domain.

Scripture quotations marked (NKJV) are taken from The Holy Bible, New King James Version®, copyright © 1979, 1980, 1982, HarperCollins. Used by permission of Thomas Nelson Publishers.

Published by

TEACH Services, Inc.
P U B L I S H I N G
www.TEACHServices.com • (800) 367-1844

Table of Contents

You Are Forgiven..........................5

What Forgiveness Is Not 11

Forgiving Someone When It Is Physically Impossible..........................23

Biblical Models of Forgiveness 31

Jesus....................................49

Bibliography 55

You Are Forgiven

"If we say that we have no sin, we deceive ourselves, and the truth is not in us. If we confess our sins, He is faithful and just to forgive us *our* sins and to cleanse us from all unrighteousness" (1 John 1:8-9, NKJV). "For all have sinned and fall short of the glory of God" (Romans 3:23, NKJV). Almost from the start of creation, humanity has been in need of forgiveness. Starting with our first parents Adam and Eve when they rebelled against their creator God and ate the forbidden fruit. Jesus has to stand in the gap on their behalf by pledging His life for their sins. He agrees to be the ransom for their sins—in reality all of humanity's sin—that is why he is "…the Lamb slain from the foundation of the world" (Revelation 13:8, KJV).

After Adam and Eve had eaten of the forbidden fruit, they were filled with a sense of shame and terror. At first their only thought was how to excuse their sin and escape the dreaded sentence of death. When the Lord inquired concerning their sin, Adam replied, laying the guilt partly upon God and partly upon his companion:

"The woman whom thou gavest to be with me, she gave me of the tree, and I did eat." The woman put the blame upon the serpent, saying, "The serpent beguiled me, and I did eat." Gen 3:12,13. (*Steps to Christ*, p. 40)

> *Almost from the start of creation, humanity has been in need of forgiveness.*

Ever since this incidence humans have been blaming others for the wrongs they have themselves committed. Human nature has not changed, has it?

Why did you make the serpent? Why did you suffer him to come into Eden? These were the questions implied in her excuse for her sin, thus charging God with the responsibility of their fall. The spirit of self-justification originated in the father of lies and has been exhibited by all the sons and daughters of Adam. Confessions of this order are not inspired by the divine Spirit and will not be acceptable to God. True repentance will lead a man to bear his guilt himself and acknowledge it without deception or hypocrisy. Like the poor publican, not lifting up so much as his eyes unto heaven, he will cry, "God be merciful to me a sinner," and those who do acknowledge their guilt will be justified, for Jesus will plead His blood in behalf of the repentant soul. (*Steps to Christ*, pp. 40, 41)

All of humanity has fallen short of God's ideal for us; we have all missed the mark. Sin has terribly preempted God's plan. It is taking a severe toll on humanity and the rest of creation. Thus, humanity is in need of forgiveness from their creator God; they are in need of a savior. His invitation and promise is "him that cometh to me I will in no wise cast out" (John 6:37, KJV). He is ever willing and ready to forgive those who ask Him for forgiveness. There is no need to carry around the weight of unforgiven sins while Jesus is so eager to forgive you of all of your sins. Jesus Christ wants to unburden you no matter how heavy your load. He invites us to "[Cast] all [our cares] upon Him for He careth for [us]" (1 Peter 5:7, KJV). Christ wants us to attain freedom. He wants us to attain abundant life, and He wants us to live life to the fullest. "I have come that they may have life, and that they may have it more abundantly" (John 10:10, KJV). That spirit of forgiveness must be exhibited among humanity. Children need to forgive their parents, parent need to forgive their children, siblings need to forgive each other, church members need to forgive their pastor, pastors needs to forgive their church members. Spouses need to forgive each other. And yes, individuals need to forgive themselves. When you repent of your sins to God and to your fellow man, you need to stop holding yourself hostage. Free yourself; release yourself in the name of Jesus. Believe and accept the promise of God's Word. "If we confess our sins, He is faithful and just to forgive us *our* sins and to cleanse us from all unrighteousness" (1 John 1:9, KJV).

"You have wounded me, but I forgive you," are simple yet profound words. These are words that convey freedom for those who utter them it is liberation from accumulated wounds. These are words that promote healing. You are giving yourself the space to start the healing process and to start realizing your God-given abilities. For far too long you have been imprisoned by your past hurt and pain, but when we choose to forgive we are creating a new beginning out of past bitterness and pain. You give yourself an opportunity to start living again. "You have hurt me deeply, but I choose to forgive you"; simple yet powerful and hopeful words that denote freedom from past misery. How refreshing are those words when uttered genuinely; they are like a refreshing drink on a hot summer day. They are like an oasis in a harsh desert. They are words that set in motion the atmosphere one needs in order to aspire to accomplish the plans God has had all along for your life, plans that were rudely preempted. You choose forgiveness because you know apart from it there is no future. Forgiveness is a deliberate decision you make to give up feelings of resentment, hurt, and a strong desire for revenge to instead to pursue a path towards peace and healing.

What Forgiveness Is Not

Forgiveness does not let the offender off the hook—the offenders should be held accountable civilly and otherwise. The relevant authorities should be notified if civil laws are broken. Forgiveness does not belittle or minimize the seriousness of the offence—the matter should be handled seriously and respectfully and there must be transparency throughout the entire process. Forgiveness does not excuse or condone what the offender did—far from it—and it is not a license to reoffend the victim and victimize others. Forgiveness does not relinquish hurtful feelings instantly; those feelings will subside with time. Forgiveness is a journey, it is not a sprint, and it is not going to happen overnight. Forgiveness does not guarantee the violator will accept the olive branch you extended to them. The ideal outcome for your offer of forgiveness is that both parties, the victim and the offender, will come away liberated from the experience. Let it be known forgiveness is primarily for the wounded person as you are unshackling yourself to start aspiring and pursuing your life goals again. Forgiveness is something you do for yourself. You are making a deliberate decision to forgive your offender, thus freeing yourself of hurt feelings, resentment, and a strong desire for revenge—regardless or not if that individual deserves it or not. Forgiveness is to bless and benefit you. You realize living a stagnant life is not a desirable trait. You are of no benefit to yourself or others living in a stuck condition. You are tired of wallowing in your past misery, so you make a self-empowering choice to emancipate yourself and press on with your life and be a productive individual.

Forgiveness is not an act of weakness; it is a self-empowering act to work up the courage and guts to tell someone who has hurt you deeply that you forgive them. I assure you forgiving someone is an act of strength—you are empowering yourself to stop being a victim and start living again. There are no benefits in holding onto unforgiveness—you are simply rehearsing your pain. Forgiveness does not necessarily mean reconciliation in every situation. It will be wise to access each situation individually as reconciliation in some situation can be downright dangerous for the victim. Reconciliation without an attempt to redeem and reform the offender is futile, and good counseling should be administered to both parties. Outside of a miracle, forgiveness does not come instantly. Deep wounds and hurt do not go away overnight, but they will when time elapses. That time will be longer or shorter for each individual. Forgive and forget is virtually impossible to do—we are living, thinking beings and some situations and circumstances are going to be reminders of past wounds. Things like sites, smells, tastes, buildings, people, and places are going to trigger your memory. You do not want to totally let your guard down; you want to maintain some skepticism. With time you will disassociate negative emotions with the memory of the event, and the hard feelings should subside along your journey to recovery. God can help you to accomplish that because, in reality, forgiveness is a gift from God to humanity. He can help you to exercise His gift successfully. "[You] can do all things through Christ which strengtheneth [you]" (Philippians 4:13, KJV).

The secular world sees forgiveness as a cultural phenomenon; they see forgiveness purely from a secular bird's-eye view. College and university researchers secularized it. The slime pit did not formulate forgiveness into existence, the big bang did not explode forgiveness into existence, chimpanzees did not initiate forgiveness into being as they have no sense of forgiveness. Forgiveness did not evolve from the bowel of evolution. Forgiveness is a divine act; it is God's gift to humanity, if you please. It is not natural for humans in their fallen state to gravitate to forgiveness when hurt is inflicted on us. The natural response is to settle the score, do not let it go, seek revenge, and let others suffer the consequences; there is a strong desire to get even without any external motivation. God gives humanity the gift of forgiveness to prevent us from destroying ourselves or our fellow man. When wounds and hurts are inflicted on us, we choose to respond in three ways: some internalize it and become an accumulator of pain and hurt thus overburdening themselves; others externalize their pain and lash out at their perpetrator; and others give up their right to be bitter and angry and the strong desire for revenge and choose the path of forgiveness, healing, and personal restoration.

Almost from the start of creation God had to exercise His gift of forgiveness to the first humans, Adam and Eve, when they rebelled against their creator and ate the forbidden fruit. They were supposed to die instantly for their rebellious act, but Jesus Christ stood in the gap by pledging His life for their sins in essence all of humanity. Jesus offered them love, mercy and forgiveness. We have to carry on the work of Jesus by being His hands, feet,

> *We have to carry on the work of Jesus by being His hands, feet, and spokesperson. We who are strong must lift up the wounded souls.*

and spokesperson. We who are strong must lift up the wounded souls. We need to perform tangible acts for those who are wounded in an effort to lift them out of their despair. We need to speak words of hope, assurance, and encouragement to them. At times we need not do anything except sit, pray, and listen as they pour out their pain and suffering. Use this to redirect them to Jesus Christ their savior who loves and cares about them. He empathizes with them and longs to restore their broken lives. We need to do whatever we can to help them along their journey to recovery "For God so loved the world that He gave His only begotten Son, that whoever believes in Him should not perish but have everlasting life" (John 3:16, NKJV). When Jesus prayed, "Father, forgive them; for they know not what they do," it was addressed to the entire human race—past, present and future (Luke 23:34, KJV). Every person who would be born was and is offered forgiveness. His gift of love, mercy, and forgiveness is available to anyone who needs it. "Him hath God exalted with His right hand to be a Prince and a Saviour, for to give repentance to Israel, and forgiveness of sins" (Acts 5:31, KJV). "To the Lord our God belong mercies and forgiveness, though we have rebelled against him" (Daniel 9:9, KJV).

Pros and Cons of Forgiveness

It has been medically proven that those who refuse to forgive and let go of hatred and grudges suffer adverse health effects such as high blood pressure, migraine headaches, heart disease, and sleep disorders. Other consequences include depression, anxiety, and lack of motivation. An unforgiving person's relationships with himself or herself and others are impacted negatively. The accumulator of pain, grudges, and hurt suffers tremendously under its weight. An unforgiving person suffers physically, emotionally, and spiritually under the weight of wounds. There is no need for us to carry those huge burdens around. Watch this! Watch this! "[Cast] all your care upon Him; for He careth for you" (1 Peter 5:7, KJV). Jesus invites us to unburden ourselves on Him—we cannot over whelm Him. He is telling us today to give Him all of our emotional turmoil, give Him your wounded heart, because Jesus is still a friend of broken hearts. The master of love, mercy and forgiveness wants us to give him all our animosity, hatred, and anger. Give Him your urge for revenge, because vengeance belongs to God and he will repay. "Come unto to me, all ye that labour and are heavy laden, and I will give you rest" (Matthew 11:28, KJV). He wants to give you peace and rest in your life, in your home. Jesus is saying to the abused one, "Give me all of your wounds, pain, hurt." He is saying to you, "Give me your emotion and confusion, and I will take them and give you healing." Yes, He will mend your broken lives. Give them all to Jesus and He will turn your weeping into joy. "Weeping may endure for a night, but joy comes in the morning" (Psalm 30:5, NKJV).

Jesus empathizes and identifies with us. He experienced a lot of the human emotions when He was on Earth. So said the prophet, "He was wounded for our transgressions, He was bruised for our iniquities; the chastisement for our peace was upon Him, and by His stripes we are healed" (Isaiah 53:5, NKJV). Sin and Satan have preempted God's plan for humanity. God meant for humans to live forever in an atmosphere of happiness and bliss. Yes, God's plan was for humans to live in paradise in an environment of love. Things like violence, hatred, jealousy, abuse, and man's inhumanity to man were not supposed to be a part of that environment. Our first parents, Adam and Eve, choose to rebel against their Creator God. Because of this, the floodgate of sin has opened, and for ages it has left a carnage of sin and destruction in its path. Untold human suffering has been inflicted on humans down through the corridor of time. People have cried out, "Why, Lord!" and "Where are you, God?" in the face of such horrendous atrocities. I am happy to tell you He is right where He has always been. God weeps with you, He understands your pain and suffering, He agonizes with you and longs to shower you with His extravagant love and compassion.

God is not the instigator of pain and suffering—Satan and demons are humanity's enemies. When they deceived our first parents, that set in motion the decline of God's creation. They here on earth fanning the flames of violence; they are spurring on man's inhumanity to man. God had to let rebellion and sin live out its ugliness for the unfallen and fallen worlds to see. Watch this: "The [Devil] does not come except to steel, and to kill, and to destroy. I have come that they may have life, and that they may have it more abundantly" (John 10:10, NKJV). God has wanted us to live vibrantly and abundantly all along. Let us read how heaven laments the casting down of Satan to the Earth: "Therefore rejoice, ye heavens, and ye that dwell in them. Woe to the inhabiters of the earth and of the sea! For the devil is come down unto you, having great wrath, because he knoweth that he hath but a short time" (Revelation 12:12, KJV). God's goal for humanity has never changed—He longs for face-to-face communion with humans like He used to have with Adam and Eve before they sinned. That is why He sent his Son, Jesus Christ, on a rescue mission to redeem humanity back to Himself. He agreed to pay the ransom for all of humanity's sins; He is "…the Lamb slain from the foundation of the world" (Revelation 13:8, KJV). That means He paid the penalty for the sins of every person who ever lived, past, present and future.

In reference to the medical knowledge mentioned earlier, when individuals choose to forgive their offenders and pursue paths of healing and personal restoration, these persons' overall health improve significantly. A lot of their sickness is reversed. For one to benefit from forgiveness it has to be genuine and heart-felt. There is nothing such as partial forgiveness; either you forgive or you do not forgive. It cannot be coerced, it must be unconditional free and complete. This is the only way you will receive the full benefit of forgiveness.

Survivors of horrendous acts are to use their experiences to bless others. When you arrive on the other side of misery, use it for greater good. The evil ones meant it for your destruction, so use it to bless others. Let your difficult experience motivate you for mission. You survive to help those who are going through similar situations. Before you could only sympathize with them; you had no clue what they endured. Now you can empathize with them; you have walked in their shoes, you have experienced what they have been through, and you are in a better position to help them. Let your wounds turn you into a warrior for good to be a blessing to others. A lot of good things have been birthed out of painful experiences. Many excellent books have been written to address atrocities that were inflicted on the authors. Many great hymns and songs were composed out of severe pain and suffering. Great organizations are formed to help victims and victimizers. Victims of abuse have decided to go back to law school and involve themselves in politics so that they can be empowered to address the problems of abuse. Individuals have dedicated their lives to prevent abuse and help victims. Places of refuge have been established to help victims of all kinds of abuse. They have let their misery motivate for mission; they are unplanned missionaries, if you please. You survive to serve and help those who going through similar situations. What the evil ones meant for your destruction, God can turn into a blessing for yourself and others. "And we know that all things work together for good to them that love God, to them who are called according to His purpose" (Romans 8:28, KJV). "'For I know the plans I have for you,' declares the Lord, 'plans to prosper you and not to harm you, plans to give you hope and a future'" (Jeremiah 29:11, NIV).

> *Let your difficult experience motivate you for mission.*

Forgiving Someone When It Is Physically Impossible

What do you do when you have lost all contact with the person you want to forgive? Perhaps you were abused when you were a child. Your abuser may have moved far away geographically, or the offence was committed at such a tender age that you could not identify your abuser, even as an adult. What do you do when the person you want to forgive is no longer in the land of the living and they are now deceased? Because forgiveness originated with God, He is the arbitrator and accreditor of forgiveness. Watch this! "For if you forgive men their trespasses, your heavenly Father will also forgive you. But if you do not forgive men their trespasses, neither will your Father forgive your trespasses" (Matthew 6:14, 15, NKJV). This holds true whether or not your offender is alive or deceased, or whether or are not you are religious. God is the manager of the gift of forgiveness. Therefore, for God to forgive us, it is incumbent on us to forgive our fellow human. God forgives us and sets us free so that we can go and free our fellow humans. The emancipated must become the emancipator;

a recipient of God's forgiveness must reciprocate that love and mercy to his or her fellow humans. "…From everyone who has been given much, much will be demanded; and from the one who has been entrusted with much, much more will be asked" (Luke 12:48, NIV).

In regard to the speech about forgiveness you would have communicated to your offender if you were able to, it is something you need to give to God. He will accredit the forgiveness to your offender. Forgiveness is not so much about your offender as it is all about you. When we choose to forgive, we turn all of grudges, hatred, and resentment to Jesus. "[Cast] all your care upon Him, for He cares for you" (1 Peter 5:7, NKJV). We are releasing ourselves and those who hurt us, and embarking on a journey of peace and healing. Of course, forgiveness is very difficult to do. That is why we have to seek the originator of forgiveness, God, for the ability and strength to forgive our offender.

> The religion of Jesus Christ means progress; it means to be ever reaching upward to a holier and higher standard. The Christian whose heart has been touched with the beauty of the

Saviour's character, is to put into practice that which he learns in the school of Christ.

Like Christ we shall forgive our enemies, and watch for opportunities to show those who have harmed us that we love their souls, and if we could, would do them good...If those who have injured us, still continue in their course of wrong-doing...we must make efforts to be reconciled to our brethren, following the Bible plan, as Christ Himself has directed. If our brethren refuse to be reconciled, then do not talk about them, nor injure their influence, but leave them in the hands of a just God, who judgeth all men righteously... (*Sons and Daughters of God*, p. 90)

"Forgive us our sins; for we also forgive every one that is indebted to us" (Luke 11:4, KJV).

Jesus teaches that we can receive forgiveness from God only as we forgive others. It is the love of God that draws us unto Him, and that love cannot touch our hearts without creating love for our brethren.

After completing the Lord's prayer, Jesus added: "If ye forgive men their trespasses, your heavenly Father will also forgive you: but if ye forgive not men their trespasses, neither will your Father forgive your trespasses." He who is unforgiving cuts off the very channel through which alone he can receive mercy from God. We should not think that unless those who have injured us confess the wrong we are justified in withholding from them our forgiveness. It is their part, no doubt, to humble their hearts by repentance and confession; but we are to have a spirit of compassion toward those who have trespassed against us, whether or not they confess their faults. However sorely they may have wounded us, we are not to cherish our grievances and sympathize with ourselves over our injuries; but as we hope to be pardoned for our offenses against God we are to pardon all who have done evil to us.

But forgiveness has a broader meaning than many suppose. When God gives the promise that He "will abundantly pardon," He adds, as if the meaning of that promise exceeded all that we could comprehend: "My thoughts are not your thoughts, neither are your ways My ways, saith the Lord. For as the heavens are higher than the earth, so are My ways higher than your ways, and My thoughts than your thoughts." Isaiah 55:7–9. God's forgiveness is not merely a judicial act by which He sets us free from condemnation. It is not only forgiveness *for* sin, but reclamation *from* sin. It is the outflow of redeeming love that transforms the heart. David had the true conception of forgiveness when he prayed, "Create in me a clean heart, O God; and renew a right spirit within me." Psalm 51:10. And again he says, "As far as the east is from the west, so far hath He removed our transgressions from us." Psalm 103:12.

God in Christ gave Himself for our sins. He suffered the cruel death of the cross, bore for us the burden of guilt, "the just for the unjust," that He might reveal to us His love and draw us to Himself. And He says, "Be ye kind one to another, tenderhearted, forgiving each other, even as God also in Christ forgave you." Ephesians 4:32, R.V. Let Christ, the divine Life, dwell in you and through you reveal the heaven-born love that will inspire hope in the hopeless and bring heaven's peace to the sin-stricken heart. As we come to God, this is the condition which meets us at the threshold, that, receiving mercy from Him, we yield ourselves to reveal His grace to others.

The one thing essential for us in order that we may receive and impart the forgiving love of God is to know and believe the love that He has to us. 1 John 4:16. Satan is working by every deception he can command, in order that we may not discern that love. He will lead us to think that our mistakes and transgressions have been so grievous that the Lord will not have respect unto our prayers and will not bless and save us. In ourselves we can see nothing but weakness, nothing to recommend us to God, and Satan tells us that it is of no use; we cannot remedy our defects of character. When we try to come to God, the enemy will whisper, It is of no use for you to pray; did not you do that evil thing? Have you not sinned against God and violated your own conscience? But we may tell the enemy that "the blood of Jesus Christ His Son cleanseth us from all sin." 1 John 1:7. When we feel that we have sinned and cannot pray, it is the time to pray. Ashamed we may be and deeply humbled, but we must pray and believe. "This is a faithful saying, and worthy of all acceptation, that Christ Jesus came into the world to save sinners; of whom I am chief." 1 Timothy 1:15. Forgiveness, reconciliation with God, comes to us, not as a reward for our works, it is not bestowed because of the merit of sinful men, but it is a gift unto us. (*Thoughts from the Mount of Blessing*, pp. 113–116)

> *The one thing essential for us in order that we may receive and impart the forgiving love of God is to know and believe the love that He has to us.*

Biblical Models of Forgiveness

The Prodigal's Father

A young man disrespectfully demanded his inheritance from his father. This was disrespectful in two ways: First, in the Jewish culture, it is dishonorable for one to ask for their inheritance before the demise of the giver and, secondly, the youngest is not to get his inheritance served first; that honor goes to the eldest son. His dad reluctantly obliged, after which the son took his inheritance and left right away to a far country, away from the scrutiny of his family and friends. He thought he was too restricted at home. While on his way he probably exclaimed, I am free now! Or so he thought. He indulged in excessive pleasure, he was the center of attraction, he was the financier of the party, and he attracted a lot of friends because of his wealth. Eventually his money ran out and there he was, penniless and friendless. As soon as his money was finished, everyone was gone. He was hungry and wore tattered clothes. He was in an emotional, physical, and spiritual wilderness. Sin devalues you, it demoralizes, and if not repented of it—it kills you. "Then when lust hath conceived, it bringeth forth sin: when it is finished, bringeth forth death" (James 1:15, KJV).

He reasoned to himself: here I am in this deplorable condition, destitute of basic necessities while my father's workers live comfortably. He decided to return to his father and ask him to accept him as a servant—not as a son—because he felt he had been too much of a disappointment. Desperate situations call for desperate solutions. His walk back home was labored and painful yet his emaciated body lumbered on, motivated by the thought that his father would show him mercy and compassion. The prodigal's father was always on the lookout for his wayward son. One day, while he was looking out in the distance, a figure caught his attention. The figure exhibited the mannerisms of his youngest son. As the person drew closer, his suspicion was confirmed. Yes, indeed it was his wayward son! The father ran towards his son with all the energy he could muster, and embraced and kissed him. He assured his son of his unconditional love and forgiveness. This father ran to his son with mercy and compassion. He welcomed him back home unconditionally as his son. The prodigal's father put on a welcoming celebration for his wayward son.

He invited people in the neighborhood to celebrate with him. He exclaimed, "This [is] my son…he was lost and is found" (Luke 15:24, NKJV).

Stephen

Head deacon Stephen was a man of God, filled with Holy Spirit, faith, and power. He was chosen to lead the group of deacons to oversee the community service program at his assembly. Stephen, under the influence of the Holy Spirit, did many evangelistic exploits for God. He wrought many miracles and wonders, he preached the word of God with power and authority and many souls were won to Christ; even priests, which enraged the priests and rulers of his day. The Sanhedrin council quickly assembled a group of false witness to judge Stephen of blasphemy. In his defense, Stephen, with all the poise and calm in the world, refuted all the false accusations brought against him. He gave them a refresher course in their history, he showed them how God lead the Israelites through the years. He pointed out their hypocrisy and forcefully showed them how their ancestors persecuted the prophets in their day, and how they are no different because they have crucified Jesus and persecuted his disciples. This infuriated them even more. This whipped them into a frenzy; they could no longer restrain their anger while he was speaking, while he was pointing out their inconsistencies, they grinded their teeth, they yelled out and rushed on him and grabbed him and pulled him outside the city and stoned him to death.

> Stephen, the foremost of the seven deacons, was a man of deep piety and broad faith. Though a Jew by birth, he spoke the Greek language and was familiar with the customs and manners of the Greeks. He therefore found opportunity to preach the gospel in the synagogues of the Greek Jews. He was very active in the cause of Christ and boldly proclaimed his faith. Learned rabbis and doctors of the law engaged in public discussion with him, confidently expecting an easy victory. But "they were not able to resist the wisdom and the spirit by which he spake." Not only did he speak in the power of the Holy Spirit, but it was plain that he was a student of the prophecies and learned in all matters of the law. He ably defended the truths that he advocated and utterly defeated his opponents. To him was the promise fulfilled, "Settle it therefore

in your hearts, not to meditate before what ye shall answer: for I will give you a mouth and wisdom, which all your adversaries shall not be able to gainsay nor resist." Luke 21:14, 15.

Because the priests and rulers could not prevail against the clear, calm wisdom of Stephen, they determined to make an example of him; and while thus satisfying their revengeful hatred, they would prevent others, through fear, from adopting his belief. Witnesses were hired to bear false testimony that they had heard him speak blasphemous words against the temple and the law. "We have heard him say," these witnesses declared, "that this Jesus of Nazareth shall destroy this place, and shall change the customs which Moses delivered us."

As Stephen stood face to face with his judges to answer to the charge of blasphemy, a holy radiance shone upon his countenance, and "all that sat in the council, looking steadfastly on him, saw his face as it had been the face of an angel." Many who beheld this light trembled and veiled their faces, but the stubborn unbelief and prejudice of

> the rulers did not waver." (*Acts of the Apostles*, pp. 97–99)

Here was a very good man of God who dedicated his gifts, talents, and abilities to advance the gospel of Jesus Christ in his sphere of influence, and he had tremendous success. The priests and religious leaders felt threatened by Stephen and the impact he was making, so they moved hastily to get rid of him. The jealousy of the religious leaders culminated into a crescendo of hatred and the man of God was thrown outside the city and stoned to death. Before the faithful man of God died, he was honored with the opportunity to see into heaven. He beheld the glory of God and he also saw his savior Jesus Christ. What a glorious privilege. Let us read more about this:

> But he, being full of the Holy Spirit, gazed into heaven and saw the glory of God, and Jesus standing at the right hand of God, and said, "Look! I see the heavens opened and the Son of Man standing at the right hand of God!" Then they cried out with a loud voice, stopped their ears, and ran at him with one accord; and they cast *him* out of the city and stoned *him*...And they stoned

Stephen as he was calling on *God* and saying, "Lord Jesus, receive my spirit." Then he knelt down and cried out with a loud voice, "Lord do not charge them with this sin." And when he had said this, he fell asleep. (Acts 7:55–60, NKJV)

A grave injustice was done to Stephen, but nevertheless in pain and with his dying breath he asked God to forgive his murderers even before they realized they needed it. Stephen then commended his spirit to God and fell asleep in death.

King David

> *... with his dying breath he asked God to forgive his murderers even before they realized they needed it.*

After King David committed adultery with Bathsheba—who then became pregnant from the affair—he subsequently arranged for her husband to be murdered. He swept the entire incident under the rug, so to speak, and expected to live in peace and happiness ever after. For a short time, King David carried on with his life as if nothing had happened. God was not happy with King David's cover-up effort. He could not let such a gross injustice to go unchallenged. That would have been a terrible example to the nation of Israel, who would have been empowered to sin, and they would have been an object of ridicule from the nation around. It would have set a bad precedent by giving the Israelites license to sin. God summoned the prophet Nathan with the responsibility to confront King David about his sins. This task had a potential to be dangerous; but Nathan, with tact, began his confrontation by telling King David a story:

> There were two men in one city, one rich and the other poor. The rich man had *exceedingly* many flocks and herds. But the poor *man* had nothing, except one little ewe lamb which he had bought and nourished; and it grew up together with him and with his children. It ate of his own food and drank from his own cup and lay in his bosom; and it was like a daughter to him. And a traveler came to the rich man, who refused to take from his own flock and from his own herd to prepare one for the wayfaring man who had come to him; but he

took the poor man's lamb and prepared it for the man who had come to him. So David's anger was greatly aroused against the man, and he said to Nathan, "*As* the Lord lives, the man who has done this shall surely die! And he shall restore fourfold for the lamb, because he did this thing and because he had no pity. Then Nathan said to David, "You *are* the man!" (2 Samuel 12:1–7, NKJV)

Lord have mercy! King David could have had him put to death as he was king with lots of power at his disposal. He could have chosen to make excuses for his sins. He could have said, "I was at a weak point in my life and the Devil overthrew me. He could have chosen to wallow in his self-pity, but instead David owned up to his wicked acts. He took responsibility for his evil acts that he had committed, he humbled himself and cried out to God in repentance, confession, and forgiveness. King David's attitude needs to be commended because he did not get defensive and retaliate against Nathan. Instead he humbled himself and asked God for forgiveness. God did forgive him for his sins. Psalm 51 is King David's very rich composition songs of confession, repentance, and assurance of forgiveness. He said things like: "Have mercy upon me, O God, according to your lovingkindness; according to the multitude of Your tender mercies, blot out my transgressions. Wash me thoroughly from my iniquity, and cleanse me from my sin" (Psalm 51:1, 2, NKJV). "Create in me a clean heart, O God, and renew a steadfast spirit within me" (Psalm 51:10, NKJV).

King David's power was given to him by God to be used justly in the confines of the law; his power was not to be used for personal exploits. God had to reprimand the king as there was too much at stake. Because of what their leader did, his subjects would have been empowered to sin unrestrained. His wicked acts denigrated his moral authority and cast a shadow over his kingly reign.

> There was a great change in David himself. He was broken in spirit by the consciousness of his sin and its far-reaching results. He felt humbled in the eyes of his subjects. His influence was weakened. Hitherto his prosperity had been attributed to his conscientious obedience to the commandments of the Lord. But now his subjects, having a knowledge of his sin, would be led to sin more freely.

His authority in his own household, his claim to respect and obedience from his sons, was weakened. A sense of his guilt kept him silent when he should have condemned sin; it made his arm feeble to execute justice in his house.

David's repentance was sincere and deep. There was no effort to palliate his crime. No desire to escape the judgements threatened, inspired his prayer. But he saw the enormity of his transgression against God; he saw the defilement of his soul; he loathed his sin. It was not for pardon only that he prayed, but for purity of heart. David did not in despair give over the struggle. In the promises of God to repentant sinners he saw the evidence of his pardon and acceptance.

This passage in David's history is full of significance to the repenting sinner. It is one the most forcible illustrations given us of the struggles and temptations of humanity, and of genuine repentance toward God and faith in our Lord Jesus Christ. Through all the ages it has proved a source of encouragement to souls that, having fallen into sin, were struggling under the burden of their guilt. Thousands of the children of God, who have been betrayed into sin, when ready to give up to despair have remembered how David's sincere repentance and confession were accepted by God, notwithstanding he suffered for his transgression; and they also have taken courage to repent and try again to walk in the way of God's commandments.

Whoever under the reproof of God will humble the soul with confession and repentance, as did David, may be sure that there is hope for him. Whoever will in faith accept God's promises, will find pardon. The Lord will never cast away one truly repentant soul. He has given this promise: "Let him take hold of My strength, that he may make peace with Me; and he shall make peace with Me." Isaiah 27:5. "Let the wicked forsake his way, and the unrighteous man his thoughts: and let him return unto the Lord, and He will have mercy upon him; and to our God, for He will *abundantly* pardon." Isaiah 55:7. (*Patriarchs and Prophets,* pp. 723, 725–726)

King David used his downfall as a teachable opportunity. When he was restored to God's favor and assurance of forgiveness and salvation he said he would "Teach transgressors Your ways, and sinners shall be converted to you" (Psalm 21:13, NKJV). What the Devil meant for bad can be used to bless others; let your mess be your ministry. The take-away from King David's downfall is that leaders should never let success in ministry get to their heads. Be warned: do not become arrogant and become careless with your relationship with God. You must be guarded and dependent on God at all times. "For in Him we live and move and have our being..." (Acts 17:28, NKJV).

Joseph

King David used his downfall as a teachable opportunity.

Joseph and his brothers were a case of sibling rivalry that went to the extreme. The hatred Joseph's brothers had for him was intense. We discovered Joseph had the gift of dreams. He dreamt several times and had a unique God-given ability to interpret dreams. His dreams were a source of contention, and every time he related his dreams to his brothers they interpreted them to mean he wanted to rule over them; even his parent accused him of this. His brothers called him "the dreamer". Joseph's father give him a beautiful coat with many colors that infuriated his brothers even more. One day when his brothers were out in the field looking after the flocks, Joseph decided to visit his brothers. When they saw him coming they said, "Look, this dreamer is coming! Come therefore, let us now kill him…" (Genesis 37:19, 20, NKJV). But Reuben, one of the older brothers, convinced them not to take his life. They eventually decided to sell him to some Ishmaelite merchants. Joseph's life took some disappointing twists and turns, and he eventually ended up in Egypt as a slave. But the Lord was with him and prospered him; his boss Potiphar rewarded his stewardship by elevating him to manager of his house. The Lord blessed the Egyptians greatly because of Joseph.

After Potiphar's wife's failed several attempts to lure Joseph into to her bed, she was enraged and falsely accused Joseph of sexually offending her. He was hastily thrown into prison and left to languish for several years. His moral excellence was on display in the prison so much so he was put in charge of the prison. Joseph's gift of dreams was instrumental to him getting out of prison and being promoted to governor in Egypt. The Egyptian king had a dream and no one in his kingdom was able to interpret his dream—except Joseph. He was quickly summoned to the palace. With God's help, Joseph was able to explain the meaning of the king's dream, and as a result, Joseph was rewarded with his freedom and a high position in the kingdom. What the evil ones meant for his downfall God turned it into a blessing. Joseph turned his misery in to a ministry. There was a severe famine in the region; food was scarce in Canaan, Joseph's home, and they received words that there was lots of food in Egypt. Jacob sent some of his sons to Egypt to purchase food where Joseph was now governor, and directly in charge of the food supplies. Joseph recognized his brothers, but they did not recognize him as he spoke Egyptian. He decided to put his brothers through a series of tests to see if they had turned from their evil ways. He heard them lamenting their abuse of him out loud. They thought they are now paying for their past wickedness towards Joseph. Joseph was emotionally overwhelmed and could not endure it any longer; it was too painful even then. He rushed out of the room to cry and composed himself. He eventually revealed himself to his brothers and they were astonished and distraught. Joseph was now in a position to inflict revenge on his brothers, but he chose instead to forgive them and pursue reconciliation. He turned his misery into a ministry. He invited his family to Egypt and took good care of them. What the Devil meant for our destruction, God uses it for good.

> The life of Joseph illustrates the life of Christ. It was envy that moved the brothers of Joseph to sell him as a slave; they hoped to prevent him from becoming greater than themselves. And when he was carried to Egypt, they flattered themselves that they were to be no more troubled with his dreams, that they had removed all possibility of their fulfillment. But their own course was overruled by God to bring about the very event that they designed to hinder. So the Jewish priests and elders were jealous of Christ, fearing that He would attract the attention of the people from them. They put Him to death, to prevent Him from becoming king, but they were thus bringing about this very result.
>
> Joseph, through his bondage in Egypt, became a savior to his father's family; yet this fact did not lessen the guilt of his brothers. So the crucifixion of Christ by

His enemies made Him the Redeemer of mankind, the Saviour of the fallen race, and Ruler over the whole world; but the crime of His murderers was just as heinous as though God's providential hand had not controlled events for His own glory and the good of man.

As Joseph was sold to the heathen by his own brothers, so Christ was sold to His bitterest enemies by one of His disciples. Joseph was falsely accused and thrust into prison because of his virtue; so Christ was despised and rejected because His righteous, self-denying life was a rebuke to sin; and though guilty of no wrong, He was condemned upon the testimony of false witnesses. And Joseph's patience and meekness under injustice and oppression, his ready forgiveness and noble benevolence toward his unnatural brothers, represent the Saviour's uncomplaining endurance of the malice and abuse of wicked men, and His forgiveness, not only of His murderers, but of all who have come to Him confessing their sins and seeking pardon. (*Patriarchs and Prophets*, pp. 239, 240)

Jesus

Jesus is the embodiment of forgiveness, the originator of forgiveness. Jesus is the master of love, mercy, and forgiveness, if you please. His life on earth was spent uplifting humanity out of their misery. He went about healing the sick, He comforted those who grieved, He miraculously fed thousands of people, and He raised the dead to life. He restored lives broken from the ravages of sin: He made the cripple walk, He restored sight to the blind, He restored speech to the dumb, and hearing to the deaf. Yes, the master of love and forgiveness freed people from demon possession and oppression. Jesus showed love in action everywhere he went; multitudes flocked to him with all kinds of sickness and disease, holding out a glimmer of hope that they were going to receive resolution to their physical and spiritual problems.

In the end, the master of love was rejected and brutalized by the people he came to save. "He came unto his own, and his own received him not" (John 1:11, KJV). Some false witnesses were assembled and a mock trial was held for the master of love our Lord and Savior Jesus Christ. He was treated like the worst of criminal; He was humiliated and abused greatly. His abuse was physical, spiritual, and emotional. He was brutally whipped beyond human comprehension and a crown of thorns was violently pressed onto his skull. His divinity was called into question: "If you are the Christ, save Yourself and us," the thief on the cross yelled (Luke 23:39, NKJV). The masses rose up in opposition against him and yelled, "Crucify Him, crucify Him!" (Luke 23:21, NKJV). Some of the people who He was near and dear to abandoned him, and some even outright denied they ever knew Him. The master of love bore the sins of the world all alone. He was finally crucified on Calvary's cross. It is said that death on the cross inflicts a slow and painful death on its victims. The prophet Isaiah, speaking about Jesus' crucifixion, says, "But he *was* wounded for our transgressions, *He was* bruised for our iniquities; the chastisement for our peace *was* upon Him; and by his stripes we are healed" (Isaiah 53:5, NKJV).

In agony and with his dying breath he said, "Father, forgive them; for they know not what they do. And they parted his raiment, and cast lots" (Luke 23:34, KJV). The penalty for all of humanity's sins was paid for by Jesus Christ. We have been great sinners, but the master of love is a greater savior. "But where sin abounded, grace did much more abound" (Romans 5:20, KJV).

What are you going through today? What is your list of pain, abuse, wounds, grudges, and more? I invite you to give it to Jesus. He sees you in your wounded and dejected state; He empathizes with you and He longs to heal your wounded soul. Let it be known He experienced some of those emotions when he was here on Earth. "The Saviour made no murmur of complaint. His face remained calm and serene, but great drops of sweat stood upon His brow… While the soldiers were doing their fearful work, Jesus prayed for His enemies, "Father, forgive them; for they know not what they do" (*The Desire of Ages*, p. 744).

"That prayer of Christ for His enemies embraced the world. It took in every sinner that had lived or should live, from the beginning of the world to the end of time. Upon all rests the guilt of crucifying the Son of God. To all, forgiveness is freely offered. "Whosoever will" may have peace with God, and inherit eternal life" (*The Desire of Ages*, p. 745). The master of love's motives are pure and noble:

He wants to restore humanity back to Himself. Ultimate restoration, healing, and peace will be realized when Jesus comes to take us out of this sinful planet and into heaven, where there will be no more pain, abuse, or suffering. The master of love, mercy, and forgiveness' invitation for you today is, "Come unto me, all ye that labour and are heavy laden, and I will give you rest" (Matthew 11:28, KJV). He wants to give you rest and peace—from all of your pain and suffering—in your heart and in your home.

> *He wants to give you rest and peace—from all of your pain and suffering—in your heart and in your home.*

No one needs to suffer under the weight of unforgiveness; no person who was hurt by his or her fellow humans needs to languish in their misery needlessly. Jesus is eager to give us peace; He invites us to unburden ourselves on Him. He is willing and eager to accept all of our burdens and replace them with a rest of soul and peace of mind. Jesus will mend our broken lives. He is well-qualified to be our burden bearer—He paid the ultimate price for all of humanity's sin when He was crucified on

Calvary's cross. He cannot wait to restore all those who remain faithful to Him, to ultimate wholeness when He comes the second time in glory. I look forward to that moment when pain and suffering will be no more and Jesus will bring an end to all of man's inhumanity to their fellowmen. "What a friend we have in Jesus, all our sins and griefs to bear."

Bibliography

White, Ellen G. *The Acts of the Apostles*. Mountain View, CA: Pacific Press Publishing Association, 1911.

White, Ellen G. *The Desire of Ages*. Mountain View, CA: Pacific Press Publishing Association, 1898.

White, Ellen G. *Patriarchs and Prophets*. Washington, DC: Review and Herald Publishing Association, 1890.

White, Ellen G. *Sons and Daughters of God*. Washington, DC: Review and Herald Publishing Association, 1955.

White, Ellen G. *Steps to Christ*. Mountain View, CA: Pacific Press Publishing Association, 1892.

White, Ellen G. *Thoughts from the Mount of Blessing*. Mountain View, CA: Pacific Press Publishing Association, 1896.

TEACH Services, Inc.
P U B L I S H I N G

We invite you to view the complete
selection of titles we publish at:
www.TEACHServices.com

We encourage you to write us
with your thoughts about this,
or any other book we publish at:
info@TEACHServices.com

TEACH Services' titles may be purchased in
bulk quantities for educational, fund-raising,
business, or promotional use.
bulksales@TEACHServices.com

Finally, if you are interested in seeing
your own book in print, please contact us at:
publishing@TEACHServices.com

We are happy to review your manuscript at no charge.

www.ingramcontent.com/pod-product-compliance
Lightning Source LLC
Chambersburg PA
CBHW042137160426
43200CB00019B/2959